The Parting

written by Diana Noonan

illustrated by Daron Parton

Stargazing

Predict

analyse the cover design and illustration and form a prediction about the content of the story and the target audience.

The night I saw the lights up at the pond was the same night that my cousin Benji received his first weird coded text message. It was 10.30 and I'd just finished setting up my telescope to check on the star that I'd been watching for the last six months. Suddenly, I thought, "Benji's going to call," and, half a second later, my mobile rumbled in my pocket.

"Fizz?"

"What's up?" I asked.

"Did you, like, just text me some weird kind of message?"

"Benji, it's Monday night. I'm stargazing, remember?"

"I know but it's just that I've had a text and it's in some kind of code. It's made up of symbols that you can't get on a mobile."

I knew he was worried about something.

"You have that strange feeling again, don't you?" I guessed. "Like you have to do something and you don't know what."

There was a silence on the other end of the phone. Then: "Can I come up to the pond?"

"Sure," I said. "But I have to keep working. There's cloud coming over and I won't have visibility for much longer."

Personal Response

"Suddenly, I thought, 'Benji's going to call'." what connections can you make to Fizz's premonition of a phone call from Benji? Do you believe in telepathic experiences? why/why not?

2

Research

HOW WOULD YOU DEVELOP A BRIEF TO research scientific evidence for the existence of telepathy?

Author Purpose

WHY DO YOU THINK THE author introduces details about a weird coded text message sent to Benji so early in the story?

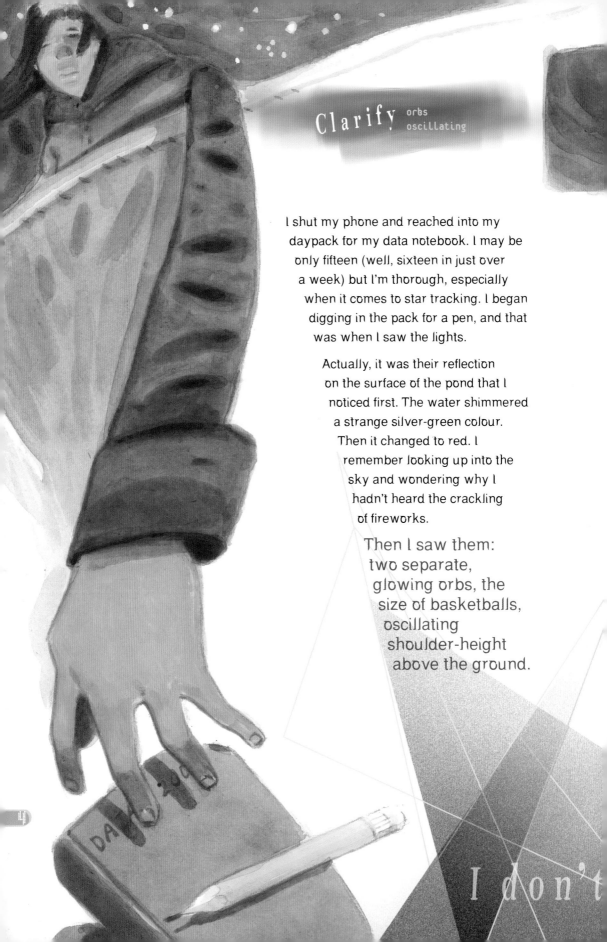

Clarify orbs oscillating

I shut my phone and reached into my daypack for my data notebook. I may be only fifteen (well, sixteen in just over a week) but I'm thorough, especially when it comes to star tracking. I began digging in the pack for a pen, and that was when I saw the lights.

Actually, it was their reflection on the surface of the pond that I noticed first. The water shimmered a strange silver-green colour. Then it changed to red. I remember looking up into the sky and wondering why I hadn't heard the crackling of fireworks.

Then I saw them: two separate, glowing orbs, the size of basketballs, oscillating shoulder-height above the ground.

I don't

They began to move and it was as though they were playing tag with each other while never shifting more than half a metre from the same spot.

I wasn't frightened. Astronomy is a serious hobby for me, so I know that ninety-nine per cent of night-light sightings are identifiable. I was more interested in capturing what I was seeing on film, so I crouched down, keeping my eyes on the lights as I reached into my bag for my camera.

Plot

why do you think fizz failed to get any photos of the orbs and could not recall the time passing? Is this significant to the development of the plot? why/why not?

All the time, I was describing to myself in detail what I was observing so that I'd be able to write up an accurate report to post on the UFO website when I got home.

The thing is, though, I don't remember time passing. It takes ten minutes to walk swiftly from Benji's house up the hill to the pond (which is what he had done) and, when he arrived, I was still on the ground, the camera in my hand (no shots taken) and the lights had gone.

"You didn't see them, did you?" I asked.

"See what?" He flicked open his phone. "This is the text," he said. "What do you think?"

Inference

what inferences can you make about fizz from factual and inferential information so far?

remember time passing...

Txt Two

The next morning at school, I sat in geography, thinking about the lights and trying to sketch them on the side of my test paper.

The hour-long test had only been in progress for fifteen minutes and already Benji and I had finished. I could see him at the front of the room, scribbling something down. He was probably trying to decipher the code that had appeared on his mobile, and I knew it wouldn't be long before he succeeded.

Benji is really smart. We both are. Our teachers don't quite know what to do with us, so we all just carry on as normal – doing the same work as everyone else, but spending most of our time thinking about other things, such as my hobby – astronomy – or Benji's – old cameras and movie equipment.

Today, though, I was also thinking a lot about what my boyfriend Jasper was going to give me for my birthday. Benji and I were having our sixteenth birthdays in a few days – we're "twin cousins". At least, that's what people call us, because we were born on the same day and our mothers, whom we've never met, were identical twin sisters.

"Benji? Felicity? Are you finished?" asked Ms Rae from the front of the class.

We nodded.

"You can go to the library and work on your assignments," she said.

I gathered my stuff and stood up. The moment we were out the door, Benji pulled his mobile from his pocket and switched it on.

"You're not supposed to bring that to school," I told him.

He stopped, stared at the screen, and then looked up at me nervously.

"I've got another one," he said. "Another one of those texts."

"Check the number it's come from."

"There isn't one," he replied.

Clarify decipher

Issues

what is your stance on
using mobile phones
in school? How do you
support your view?

Personal Response

why do you think Benji is
concerned about the text
message? what would you
do if you received a text
message like this?

...I've got another
one of those texts

He looked around, agitated, as though he couldn't decide what to do. Then he said the strangest thing.

"If – if I could just go to the pond, I think I'd know what to do. I think I'd be able to crack the code."

Benji and I don't talk a lot about the pond where I go to study the stars, even though it's a special place for us. It's on the farm where we live; on the land that our dads, who are brothers, own in partnership. Ever since we've been old enough to go places by ourselves, we've spent a lot of time up there, just mucking around.

why has the author introduced a hesitation when Benji says, "If – if I could just go to the pond..."? what does this indicate?

Language Feature

The pond's not anything special to look at: it's just a pool of water about thirty metres long that the cattle go to drink from. Our dads made it before we were born by bulldozing a dam across a stream. Sometimes there are ducks swimming on it and, once, a heron made its nest there in a tree above the reeds.

...the pond is a special place for us

Issues

what issues surround skipping school? what would you say to Benji about his taking off to the pond?

You can't swim in the pond. It's deep and there are dead trees under the water, so it would be really easy to get caught on a snag and drown.

Inference

"I've got to go to the pond and figure out this code."

Is there an underlying reason why Benji is drawn to the pond? What inferences can you make about this?

That's what our dads have always told us. So Benji and I just meet up there and hang around the place, skipping stones, talking, maybe making a fire. We've camped up there a few times, too. Lately, Benji has made me promise never to take Jasper there. I don't know exactly why he said that, or why I agreed.

"I'm going home," said Benji suddenly. "I've got to go to the pond and figure out this code. Come with me, Fizz."

I stared at him and shook my head.

"I'm not skipping school," I told him. "And neither should you."

"I know," said Benji weakly. "But I have to. I just have to, Fizz."

Was the author's description of the setting effective in helping you form a visual image of the pond? Why/why not?

Setting

9

Mystery Girls

When I got home from school, Dad and Uncle Luke were working together on one of the farm tractors. They didn't say anything about Benji, so I knew they hadn't seen him arrive home early.

"Anything special happen at school?" asked Dad, his head inside the engine.

"Not really," I said. Then I remembered the newsletter in my bag. "Oh, that's right, we're having a school fair at the end of the month. Our class is running an auction. We have to bring along any old stuff from home that's not wanted."

Uncle Luke looked around the shed. "Plenty of bits and pieces here," he said with a chuckle.

He was absolutely right. Dad and Uncle Luke are real hoarders. They've lived on the farm all their lives and collected stuff since they were kids.

Sometimes Benji and I wonder if that's what drove our mothers away.

Clarify free spirits

But that's not true, of course. We don't really know why they left when Benji and I were just one year old. Dad and Uncle Luke say it was because they were "free spirits" – hippy sort of people. They just arrived one day, asking for work on the farm, and eventually they ended up marrying our dads. People in town called them the "mystery girls", because they never saw them. They say our mums never left the farm, not even to have their babies, which I know is true because Benji and I were both born at home.

Inference

"People in town called them the 'mystery girls', because they never saw them."

what inferences can you make about the reasons why the "mystery girls" never went off the farm and were never seen by the community?

Plot

Is the author pushing the
boundaries of credibility
in your view by having Fizz
and Benji born on the same
day, and both with mothers
who Left? why/why not?

11

Question

what do you think
happened to the mothers?

I could spend my whole life thinking about my mum and wishing she'd stayed, but I don't because there's no point. She left and so did Benji's mum. That's what happens to families sometimes and you can wonder and wonder, but in the end you just have to accept it. Anyway, I've got Dad, and he and I are best friends.

"I thought I might check out the old house for things that could be auctioned," I said. "There might still be plates and things in there. Some of that old stuff is worth a lot now."

Dad pulled his head out of the engine in a hurry, but I already knew I'd said something wrong, because Uncle Luke was staring at me.

"Don't go into the old house," said Dad. "We've told you before, it's dangerous."

Dad and Uncle Luke were brought up in the old house on the farm. They lived there until their parents died and for a few months after they got married – while their new houses were being built. Then the old house caught fire and now they say that what's left standing could collapse at any time.

I'd heard it all before, of course. Only now I really wanted to go inside it.

"I'm going to get changed and then head up to the pond," I told Dad.

"Haven't you got homework?"

"I'm only going up for half an hour."

12

Tone of voice

How does the author show
Fizz's change of mood
through her choice of
language? What effect
does this have?

Language Feature

Beyond the Text

what connections can you make to fizz's experience with an **indescribable force**? are there other indescribable forces in books/movies you have read/seen? were they similar/dissimilar?

Dad and Uncle Luke looked at me, like they always do when I mention the pond, as though they don't want me to go there, but can't think of a reason why I shouldn't. I guess I've got so used to it over the years that I hardly notice, but today something felt different. It was like an indescribable force, as though something inside of me was saying to them, "Don't tell me what to do."

And it wasn't just about the pond. It was about the old house as well. I knew right then, while they were still looking at me, that I would always go to the pond and that I was going to go into the old house, too. I knew that those were things I had to do. I didn't have a choice.

"Fizz?" said Dad. It was as if his voice came from a long way off.

"What?"

"Be careful up there. Don't go in the water."

Reading Between the Lines

fizz feels that her father and uncle don't like her going to the pond but have no real reason to forbid it. what do you think is the context for their reluctance?

Homesick

Benji was up at the pond when I got there, hunched over a notebook with a pen in his hand.

"I can see a pattern in the symbols," he said, before he'd even turned round. He sounded upset. "But I can't figure out what they say."

"Maybe you don't have to," I offered. "Maybe it's not important. It might just be some kind of joke."

Suddenly, Benji's shoulders started shaking. He was crying – something I hadn't seen him do since we were really little.

"Benji?" I put my arm around his shoulders, but he pulled away.

"What's wrong with me?" he asked, still crying.

"I'm so tired of this feeling I keep getting."

"The have-to-do-something feeling?"

He shook his head. "Not just that. I have this hollow, lonely kind of...sadness inside me. It's been there for a couple of weeks now. It's like I want to...to..."

He looked up at me with this strange, lost expression on his face. "I feel really, really homesick," he said. "But I'm here on the farm, with you and Uncle Ferg and Dad. So I already *am* home – aren't I?"

I didn't know what to say. I thought that maybe I'd tell Uncle Luke that Benji should talk to the school counsellor. I sat beside him for a while, then stood up and started biffing stones into the pond. Benji joined me and I told him about the auction and my idea of going to the old house to look for stuff.

"Sure," he said. "Let's do that."

The old house is behind a stand of big macrocarpa trees that the cattle like to shelter under on rainy days. You can't see it from Benji's house or mine, or from the shed where Dad and Uncle Luke were working.

14

Reading Between the Lines

why do you think benji feels homesick when he is already home? what do you think lies behind this?

Personal Response

"I have this hollow, lonely kind of…sadness inside me."
what feelings did Benji's sadness evoke in you? if you were Fizz, how would you comfort him?

Issues

15

what safety issues arise from going into a derelict building affected by fire?

I pushed the front door open with the toe of my boot and we looked down the charred hallway with thistles growing up where the floorboards used to be.

"This is a waste of time," said Benji after we'd peered into a couple of the rooms where the roof hadn't fallen in. "And Dad and Uncle Ferg are right. It *is* dangerous."

Clarify charred super-8 movie

"What's that?" I asked. I was looking at a rusting tin trunk lying on its side under some pieces of broken window. Benji went over to it and kicked the glass aside.

"All rusted up," he said, tugging at the catch.

He turned to go out of the house, but I was still looking at the trunk. My farm boots are heavy old things with a metal toecap, so I kicked the catch hard and it broke off and went flying across the room.

"What's in it?" asked Benji, looking back.

I crouched over the contents: a couple of mouldy paintings falling out of their frames and some old, mildew-covered calendars.

Opinion

what is your opinion about fizz and benji going into the old house? what would you say to them?

...this is a waste

Plot

what do you think
will happen now in the
storyline? is the old
super-8 movie a significant
development in the plot?
what do you think might
be on the tape?

"Nothing," I said. "Just junk." I picked up a plastic reel with stuff a bit like cassette tape wound around it and held it up to the light.

"What's this?" I asked and, instantly, Benji was beside me.

"It's an old super-8 movie," he said, sounding more alive than he'd been in ages. "Hey, I could use my projector to play it. That'd be cool."

"You think it'll be playable?" I asked. "It looks pretty old."

Benji took it from my hands and began winding up the tape that was spilling off the reel. "I'll give it a go," he said.

Question Generate

what questions could
you ask about the
discovery of the
super-8 movie reel?

17

of time...

The Super-8

Benji and I didn't see each other much the next week because he didn't come to school. When I phoned him, he said that he felt too miserable and that he'd told his dad he had the flu. He'd also received two more texts and he was having some weird dreams.

"What sort of dreams?" I asked, but he wouldn't tell me.

Some pretty strange things were happening to me, too, but they interested more than upset me.

Clarify a bad space

First, there were the lights. I saw them up at the pond again, hovering and playing tag with each other across the water. I still wasn't scared of them – at least not until they began to move towards me. I backed away but, as they got closer, they seemed to hum. What was truly weird was that I found myself speaking to them, saying, "What do you want?", because I really felt that they wanted to make some kind of contact with me.

I would have told Benji all this – he's the only person I would have told – but I didn't think I should because he was in such a bad space. Maybe I could have told Jasper, but he and I were getting along so well and I didn't want him to think I was crazy.

What happened after that was actually very frightening. It started in class. Usually, I have no trouble answering questions. In fact, I'm the first to answer and I'm always right. But on Tuesday I started getting "blocks". That's the only way I can describe them. The teacher would ask a question and it was as though I couldn't hear her because of this noise.

It was a high-pitched screech like the sound of a dial-up Internet connection. It made me cover my ears, which was hopeless because the sound was inside my head. I had to go to the sick bay, but the noise wouldn't leave me so, in the end, one of the teachers drove me home.

Benji must have seen me arrive because, as soon as I was inside, he phoned.

"Fizz," he said. "Come up to the house. Come quick. I've got something to show you."

19

Uncle Luke and Dad had gone to a cattle sale, so the house was empty except for Benji, who was sitting in the basement where he shows his films. He looked good – happy and sort of excited.

"Sit down," he said. "Watch this."

He dimmed the lights and switched on the projector.

"This is the super-8 you found up at the old house."

The picture was scratched and there was no sound.

"It's up at the pond," I said, recognising the trees.

"And the dam's just been built," said Benji. "Look, the clay is still fresh."

Two figures in bikinis, their backs to the camera, came into shot, heading for the water. My heart leapt. Benji and I had never seen a picture of our mothers. Dad and Uncle Luke had said that all the photos had been burned in the house fire.

"Wait!" I said. "There's something wrong with them. Stop the film, Benji. Pause it."

He couldn't. Super-8 movies don't work like that, but he didn't need to for me to see that the two women on the screen had unnatural, impossibly tiny waists. It was as though their bodies were made up of two separate parts, joined in the middle the way the abdomen of an insect is joined to its thorax.

Plot

HOW WOULD THE STORY BE DIFFERENT IF THE SUPER-8 MOVIE HAD NOT BEEN FOUND?

there's something wrong with them

Reading Between the Lines

"Dad and Uncle Luke had said that all the photos [of our two mothers] had been burned in the house fire."

WHY DO YOU THINK THEY SAID THIS? DO YOU THINK THIS REVEALS SOME SINISTER MOTIVE ON THEIR PART? WHY/WHY NOT?

what interpretational
consequences does the
illustration have for
the story?

Reading Between the Lines

why do you think fizz felt sick when she saw her
father put his arm around one of the creatures?

Analyse

why were the reactions of Fizz and Benji to the pictures of their mothers so different?

I started to say something, but Benji held up his hand. "Wait," he said. "Watch this."

The next moment, the two women turned back to wave to the person holding the camera, and that was when I saw their identical faces.

Their almond-shaped eyes stretched from the middle of their hollow cheeks to their protruding foreheads and their mouths were dark holes beneath flattened noses.

I started to say that these hideous, alien creatures were not our mothers, that they were nothing to do with us, but suddenly my dad came into shot, laughing, and wrapped his arm around the shoulders of one of them.

Turn it off!
Stop the film!

I felt sick. "Turn it off!" I shouted. "Stop the film!"

But Benji's eyes were fixed firmly on the screen.

"They're so beautiful," he said. "Our mothers, they're so beautiful."

After that, we sat watching the rest of the reel: the long shot of Uncle Luke pushing something closer and closer towards the edge of the pool with the blade of the tractor, until whatever it was toppled over, rolled a couple of times and disappeared under the water. Then the screen went black.

Inference

"I'm taking the digger. I'm going to break the dam. It's what they want us to do."

what inferences can you make from this about Benji's intentions?

"Let's go," said Benji.

"Go where?"

"Up to the pond. I'm taking the digger. I'm going to break the dam."

"You can't!" I told him.

"I have to," he said. "It's what they want us to do."

Predict

what do you think Uncle Luke pushed into the pond?

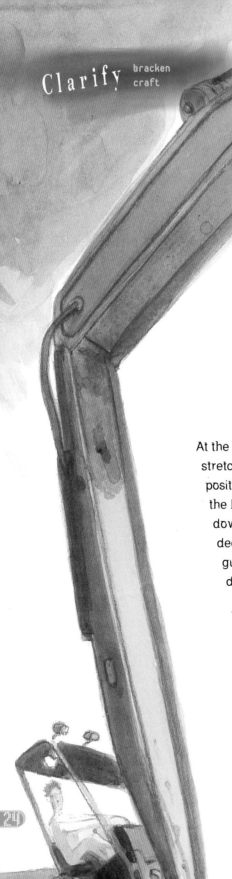

Clarify bracken craft

The Pond

Benji's been driving the digger since he was twelve years old. He knows exactly what to do. He backed it out of the shed, and I followed, walking behind as he drove it slowly up the hill.

At the pond, he manoeuvred the digger through a stretch of bracken and fern until its tracks were positioned at the edge of the water. The next minute, the bucket arm of the machine stretched out and down and gouged again and again at the clay until a deep channel had been cut through the dam. Water gushed out of the pond, turning orange as it spilled down into the creek.

After a few minutes, Benji jumped down from the cab and landed beside me.

"Look!" he said, pointing to something metallic slowly appearing in the middle of the pond as the water drained away.

"Not a speck of rust," said Benji. "What kind of metal do you think it is?"

Author Purpose

"Not a speck of rust," said Benji. "What kind of metal do you think it is?"

why does the author include this description?

24

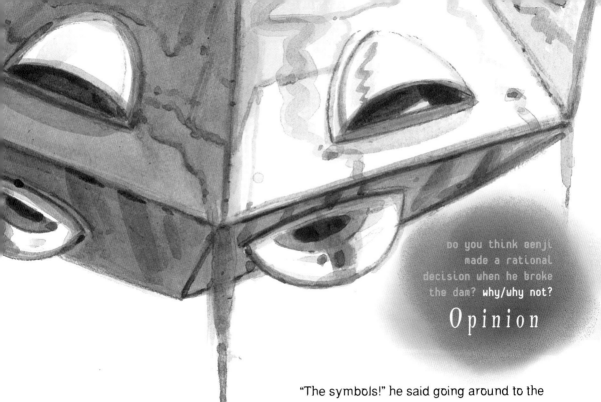

Do you think Benji made a rational decision when he broke the dam? why/why not?

Opinion

I shook my head and Benji started climbing back up into the cab of the digger.

"What are you doing?"

He spun the digger around and worked levers so that its arm reached out over the water and the teeth of its bucket caught on the metal object and lifted it.

It was a hexagonal machine, a vehicle of some sort.

Muddy water spilled out of it as Benji set it down on the grass beside the pond. Then he switched off the engine of the digger and came around to look at the thing.

"The symbols!" he said going around to the other side of it. "Look, on the side of the craft. They're the same as the ones in my text messages."

I stared at him. I felt scared.

"It's what they arrived in – our mothers," he said. "Those messages on my mobile, they're from my mother. She wants me, Fizz. She wants me to go home."

I opened my mouth to say that he'd got it wrong, but now the lights were there, the orbs, and they were playing around the strange craft, ducking and diving in and out of it, humming.

Benji opened the door of the vehicle and stepped into it.

Reading Between the Lines

Why did Fizz feel scared when the symbols on the hexagonal craft matched the symbols in the strange text messages?

Plot

Has the plot
been convincing/
unconvincing in
your opinion?
Why/why not?

"What are you doing? Benji!"

He didn't answer and now I was screaming at him. "Benji!"

"You don't understand," he said. "It's too hard for me to stay here. It hurts to stay."

The lights bobbed and danced, and it was no longer them humming, but the craft.

"You can't do this!" I shouted at Benji, because now I knew exactly what was going to happen. "You can't leave your dad. You can't leave me!"

"Come with me, Fizz. I'm going home." He stretched out his arm, but I stepped back. Now the lights were circling me, trying to drive me into the craft with Benji. And the terrible thing was that, in some way, I did want to go. In that instant, I so much wanted to be with the mother I had never met that I almost took Benji's hand.

It started to rain then, and a patch of watery sunlight stretched down from a gap in the cloud, so that all the bush around the pond shimmered. I heard the birds call from the trees, as they do at the start of a rain storm, and I looked down the hill over our farm where I was born and had spent all my life, and along the green valley that stretches out towards school and town. I thought of my dad and Jasper and being sixteen tomorrow with all my friends around me.

Personal Response

"I'm going home."
what feelings are evoked
by Benji's realisation?
How would you feel if
you were Fizz?

stay ...

"Please don't go," I begged Benji. But I knew that it was the lights that I was talking to as well. "Please, don't go."

The hum grew louder. The craft, still dripping pond water, lifted slightly and hovered above the ground, the lights now beneath it, supporting it.

When it was twenty metres up in the air, Benji looked down at me, but I barely recognised him. His mouth was a dark, empty space and tears were falling from his almond eyes.

I watched until the craft was only a speck in the sky. Then I turned to go back down the hill. By now my father and Uncle Luke would be home. Perhaps they had already found the movie and were watching it, and I would have little to explain.

27

Beyond the Text
If there were a sequel to this story, what might you include?

Think about
the Text

Making Connections

what connections can you make to the characters,
plot, setting and themes of The Parting?

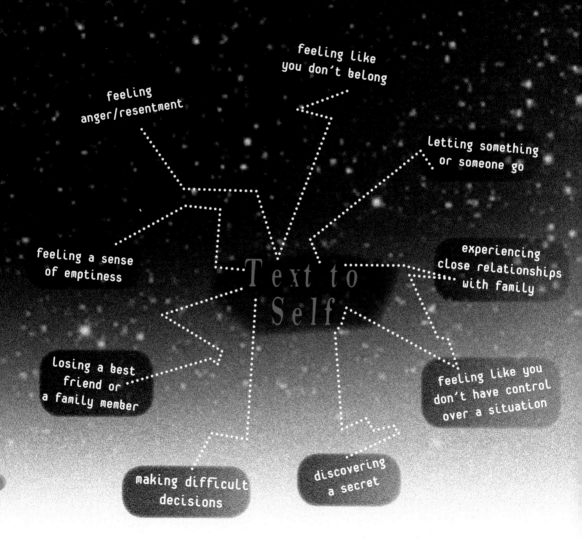

feeling like
you don't belong

feeling
anger/resentment

letting something
or someone go

feeling a sense
of emptiness

experiencing
close relationships
with family

Text to
Self

losing a best
friend or
a family member

feeling like you
don't have control
over a situation

making difficult
decisions

discovering
a secret

Text to Text/Media

Talk about texts/media you have read, listened to or seen that have similar themes and compare the treatment of theme and the differing author styles.

Text to World

Talk about situations in the world that might connect to elements in the story.

Planning a
Science-fiction
Story

Think about what defines science fiction.
Science fiction is set in an imaginary world of the future,
or a world that contains futuristic elements unknown in
our present time frame. The situations and events feature
scientifically advanced phenomena that are more or less
feasible.

1 Think about the Plot

Introduce an event involving futuristic elements unknown in our present
time frame that presents a problem or conflict and bring in the
characters that the event affects.

Decide on an event
to draw the reader
into your story.
What will the main
conflict/problem be?

Build your story to
a turning point.
This is the most
exciting/suspenseful
part of the story.

climax

Rising Action

Falling Action

conflict

Decide on a final
event that will
resolve the conflict/
problem and bring your
story to a close.

Set the scene:
who is the
story about?
when and where
is it set?

introduction

resolution

2   Think about the Characters

how characters think, feel and act as they respond to
events/situations that suggest an alien world

what might motivate their behaviour

what kind of unknown or extraterrestrial elements their
world incorporates: for example, subconscious communication,
the ability to travel to another time/place...

- the social/circumstantial structures that
typecast the characters' status, appearance
and behaviour.

3   Decide on the Setting

Atmosphere/mood   ⟶   Location   time

use predictions of scientific advances and your
imagination to make your setting feasible.

Writing a
Science-fiction
Story

Have you...

- exposed the hopes and anxieties of characters in unforeseen situations that relate to a futuristic/alien world?

- been true to the context of your time frame?

- provided a window on the future/alien world?

- explored the values and beliefs of another time or place?

- developed events that might be feasible?

- used scientific "dressing" to clothe the fantasy content?

...don't forget to revisit your writing

Do you need to change, add or delete anything to improve your story?